···A **TIMELINE HISTORY** OF THE ···
TRANSCONTINENTAL RAILROAD

· **TIMELINE TRACKERS** : WESTWARD EXPANSION · ·

ALISON BEHNKE

Lerner Publications ◆ Minneapolis

CONTENTS

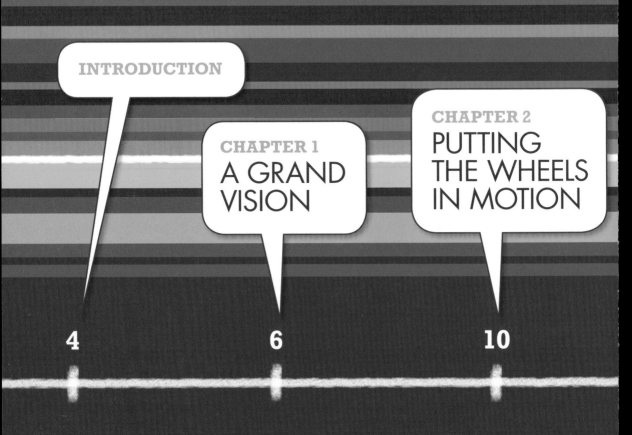

Lerner Publications Company
A division of Lerner Publishing Group, Inc.
241 First Avenue North
Minneapolis, MN 55401 USA

For reading levels and more information, look up this title at www.lernerbooks.com.

Library of Congress Cataloging-in-Publication Data

Behnke, Alison.
  A timeline history of the transcontinental railroad / by Alison Marie Behnke.
    pages cm. — (Timeline trackers: Westward expansion)
  Audience: Ages 10 to 14.
  Includes bibliographical references and index.
  ISBN 978-1-4677-8581-5 (hardback : alkaline paper) —
  ISBN 978-1-4677-8642-3 (paperback : alkaline paper) —
  ISBN 978-1-4677-8643-0 (ebook PDF)
  1. Pacific railroads—History—Juvenile literature.
2. Railroads—West (U.S.)—History—Juvenile literature.
3. Railroads—United States—History—Juvenile literature.
4. Railroads—United States—Design and construction—History—Juvenile literature. 5. United States—Territorial expansion—Juvenile literature. I. Title.
F865.W365 2015
979.4'04—dc23   2014041987

Manufactured in the United States of America
1 – BP – 7/15/15

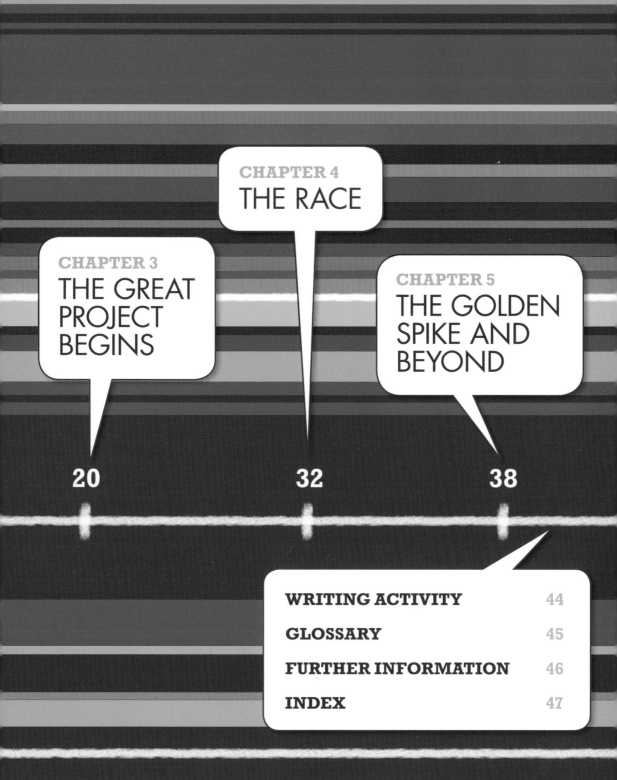

COVER PHOTO:
Central Pacific Railroad workers lay tracks in Nevada.

INTRODUCTION

The map of the United States has not always looked the way it does in modern times. In the early nineteenth century, most western states were not yet part of the country.

But many people in the United States dreamed of settling the huge area west of the Mississippi River. By the mid-nineteenth century, the country had the tools to begin making that dream come true. Some of those tools had come out of the Industrial Revolution. This historical period started in England around 1760. It brought huge changes. Scientists and inventors made machines to do many jobs that people had previously done by hand. The Industrial Revolution brought new ways to farm, make goods, and more. It touched almost every part of human life.

One new invention was the steam locomotive. This machine would power the trains of the nineteenth century. By then the United States was already building railroads in the East. But people wanted more of them. Gradually, a bold idea took shape: a single railroad connecting the East and the West. This huge rail line would stretch from the Atlantic Ocean to the Pacific Ocean. Spanning North America, it would be the first railway to cross a continent: the first transcontinental railroad.

The US transcontinental railroad made history. It would take more than six years, tens of millions of dollars, and tens of thousands of workers to build. And in the United States, it would change travel, trade, and life forever.

TIMELINES

In this book, a series of dates and important events appear in timelines. Timelines are a visual way of showing a series of events over a time period. A timeline often reveals the cause and effect of events. It can help explain how one moment in history leads to the next. The timelines in this book display important turning points surrounding the building of the first transcontinental railroad. Each timeline is marked with different intervals of time, depending on how close together events happened. Solid lines in the timelines indicate regular intervals of time. Dashed lines represent bigger jumps in time.

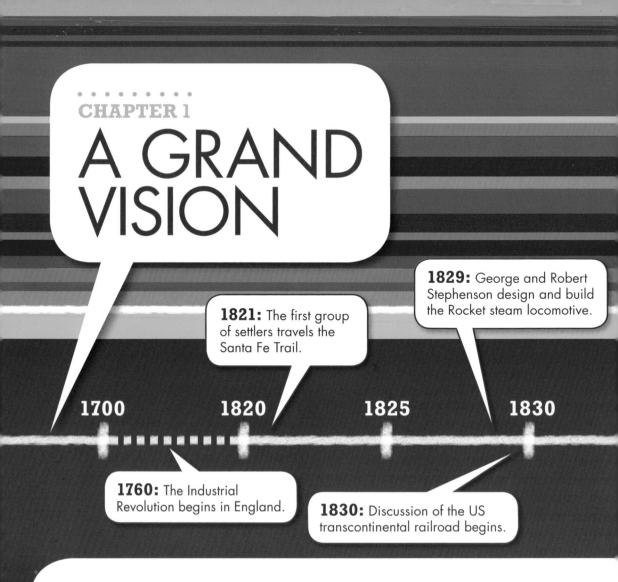

CHAPTER 1

A GRAND VISION

1829: George and Robert Stephenson design and build the Rocket steam locomotive.

1821: The first group of settlers travels the Santa Fe Trail.

1700   1820   1825   1830

1760: The Industrial Revolution begins in England.

1830: Discussion of the US transcontinental railroad begins.

The Industrial Revolution brought changes to the way people lived, worked, and traveled.

In 1829 a British engineer named George Stephenson and his son, Robert, built a steam locomotive. They called it the Rocket. Its power came from a steam engine. On a moving train, workers shoveled coal or wood into the engine to feed a large fire. Hot air from the fire went into pipes that traveled through a tank of water. These pipes heated the water, making steam. The engine used that steam to create energy. And this energy turned the train's wheels.

Trains and railroads had existed before the Rocket. Very early trains were carts pulled by horses along tracks. Steam locomotives first appeared in England around 1804. But the Rocket was faster and more efficient than others.

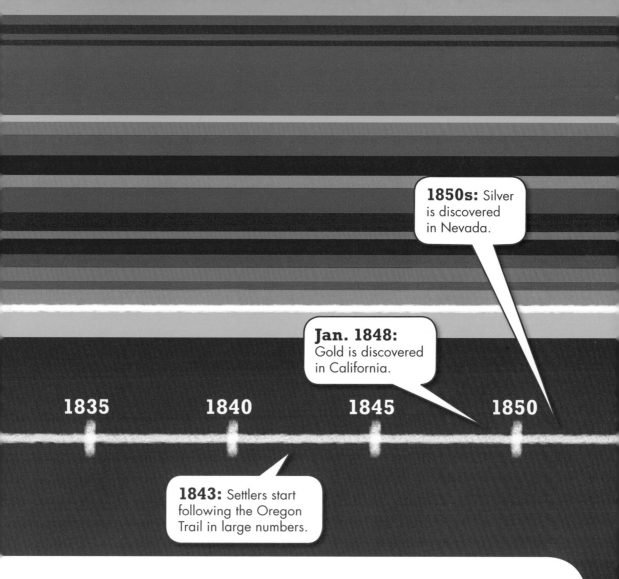

1850s: Silver is discovered in Nevada.

Jan. 1848: Gold is discovered in California.

1835   1840   1845   1850

1843: Settlers start following the Oregon Trail in large numbers.

A Better Way to Travel

Locomotive fever soon spread to the United States. By 1830 politicians, engineers, and business owners were talking about building a railroad to the Pacific Ocean.

As the country added more territory, it needed better ways to move people and products across long distances. In the early and mid-nineteenth century, the main forms of traveling over land were by horse and by wagon. But each method had drawbacks. Bad weather made traveling by horse difficult. Besides, horses need rest. They can get sick or hurt. The same goes for oxen, which often pulled wagons.

Travel could also be dangerous. Covered wagons did not offer much shelter. Riding on horseback offered none at all.

Travelers often became sick. Bad weather killed people and animals. Accidents could delay travel and hurt or kill travelers.

In some regions, settlers faced resistance from American Indians. Hundreds of different groups lived across the country. Many lived on the land that newer Americans were traveling through and settling. Sometimes these American Indians helped settlers. American Indians offered food, shelter, or directions. But American Indians also clashed with settlers. Many white settlers heading West brought threats, including guns and sickness. Contact with white settlers often threatened American Indians' way of life—and even their lives. Some American Indians were killed. Others were enslaved. American Indians, fearful of such possibilities, sometimes robbed or killed travelers before travelers could harm them.

With these challenges and more, a trip to the West Coast took a long time. Many travelers started in Missouri, where they could buy supplies. The trip from there to the West Coast

Settlers traveling by wagon faced many hardships, including bad weather, sickness, travel delays, and accidents.

often lasted four to six months. And it was costly. Not everyone could afford the horses, oxen, wagons, and other necessary goods. The idea of a train to replace this trek was exciting.

Why Go West?

For many reasons, hundreds of thousands of people journeyed west in the early and mid-nineteenth century in spite of all the risks. Some people were seeking religious freedom. Others had escaped slavery and sought their freedom in the West. And many hoped for a chance to make a better living.

Most westward travelers were looking for better lives, bigger opportunities, and a bit of adventure. The West seemed to offer all of that. It had great potential for farming, logging, hunting, and mining.

People making the trip took different routes. Some went southwest, along the Santa Fe Trail. Many other people followed the Oregon and California Trails.

Then, in 1848, gold was found in California. The California gold rush began in 1849. Thousands of people went west hoping to strike it rich. Another big discovery followed in the 1850s, when a huge source of silver was found in Nevada. More people than ever wanted to head west. Talk of a railroad grew louder.

And some people saw a bigger picture. They imagined a land whose people truly felt like one. With a railroad from coast to coast, the young nation would be connected in a new and powerful way.

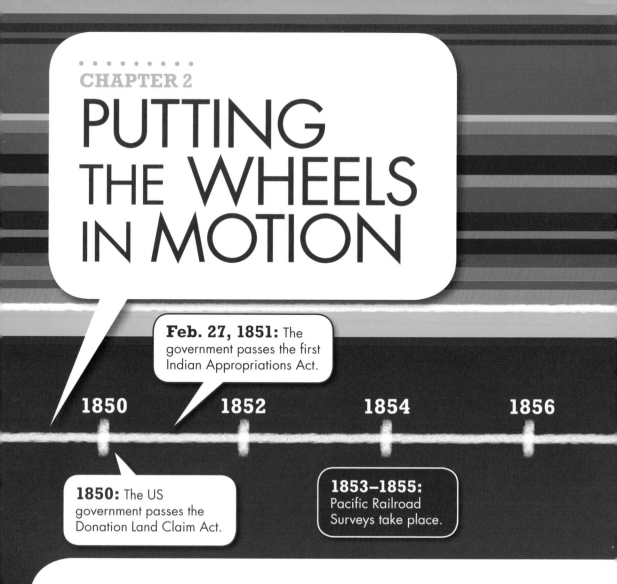

CHAPTER 2

PUTTING THE WHEELS IN MOTION

Feb. 27, 1851: The government passes the first Indian Appropriations Act.

1850 1852 1854 1856

1850: The US government passes the Donation Land Claim Act.

1853–1855: Pacific Railroad Surveys take place.

The idea of the railroad had taken hold. But making the dream a reality was the real challenge. One big question was what route the railroad would take. This would not be just a practical decision. It was also political.

At the time, the country was deeply divided on the issue of slavery. In southern states, slavery was legal. Enslaved people of African descent were forced to work in fields and homes. Most lived in terrible conditions. Northern states had outlawed slavery by the 1820s. As new states and territories joined the country, some made slavery illegal. Others allowed slavery.

Many northern politicians and citizens wanted slavery outlawed nationwide. Southerners said that states should decide for themselves. The long and bitter debate affected plans for the railroad. Southern politicians and business

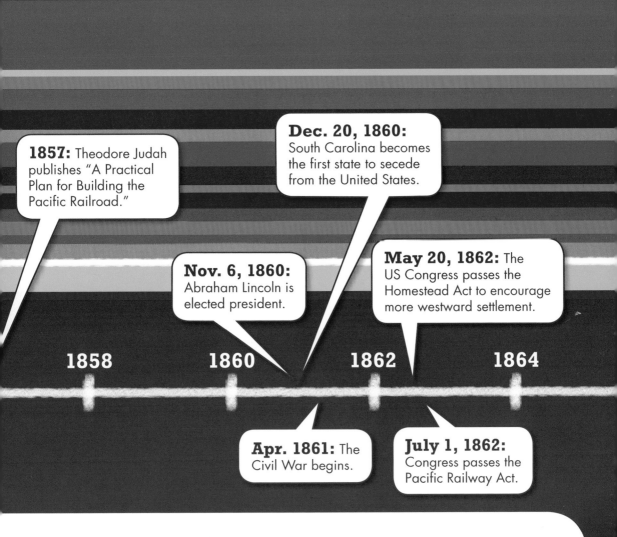

1857: Theodore Judah publishes "A Practical Plan for Building the Pacific Railroad."

Dec. 20, 1860: South Carolina becomes the first state to secede from the United States.

Nov. 6, 1860: Abraham Lincoln is elected president.

May 20, 1862: The US Congress passes the Homestead Act to encourage more westward settlement.

1858   1860   1862   1864

Apr. 1861: The Civil War begins.

July 1, 1862: Congress passes the Pacific Railway Act.

owners wanted the track to go through slaveholding states. Northerners wanted the opposite.

Clearing a Path

The railroad's path would also affect American Indians. Many of them lived on the land the tracks would cross. The US government was determined to control this land. US leaders saw American Indian communities as a threat to their plans. As the United States took over new territories, the government signed treaties with different groups of American Indians all across the country. Some of these agreements were aimed at ending American Indian attacks on settlers. Some allowed the US government to build roads across the western plains. Others arranged for American Indians to trade land for money.

US leaders also encouraged white people to settle lands where American Indians lived. In 1850 Congress passed the Donation Land Claim Act. This law said that certain types of people who were willing to settle in Oregon Territory could claim plots of land. In exchange for the land, settlers had to farm there for four years.

Then the US government decided to go yet another step further. One February 27, 1851, Congress passed a new law. The Indian Appropriations Act said that the government had the power to move American Indians onto reservations in Oklahoma. This relocation would not happen all at once. But politicians used the law to prepare for building the railroad. And for the tens of thousands of American Indians who were forced onto reservations, relocation threatened cultures that had existed for centuries.

The 1851 Indian Appropriations Act was not the first time the US government had pressured American Indians to move. In 1838 the government forced Cherokee people east of the Mississippi River to move west, in a migration known as the Trail of Tears.

Which Way to the Sea?

Meanwhile, debates about the railroad's route raged on. So Congress set aside money for government surveys of the West. Their goal was to finally choose a path. The surveys would consider how easy or difficult the land would be to build on. They also studied how regional weather might affect travel.

In 1853 the Pacific Railroad Surveys began. Surveying teams included engineers, explorers, scientists, mapmakers, and artists. These teams studied possible routes for the railroad. The paths included one in the north, two central routes, and two southern routes.

The surveys lasted until 1855. Surveying teams looked at more than geography. They learned about animals and plants in the West. They recorded information about geology. Surveyors collected rocks and fossils. And they described American Indian groups living in the area.

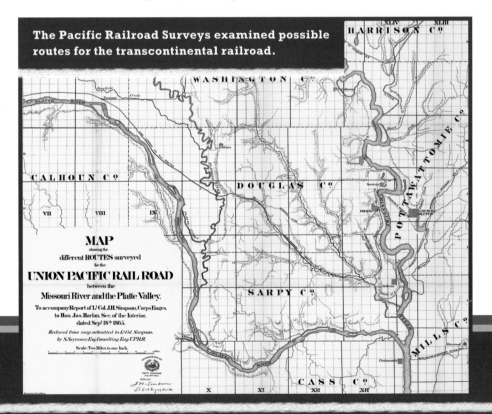

The Pacific Railroad Surveys examined possible routes for the transcontinental railroad.

What the surveys did not find was a single best route for the railroad. The good news was that it seemed as if several different routes could work. The bad news was that two years of work brought the country no closer to a plan.

Crazy Judah

Meanwhile, one man went ahead with his own plan. Theodore Judah was a railroad engineer. In 1854 he moved to California to work on the new Sacramento Valley Railroad. He soon became a major voice in the call for the transcontinental railroad.

Judah talked to politicians in California about supporting the railroad. And he tackled one of the biggest barriers to a railroad route: the Sierra Nevada. Most people thought it

Most people thought building a railroad over the rugged Sierra Nevada would be impossible.

would be impossible to build tracks through this steep, rocky mountain range. Still, Judah believed he could find a way to make it work. He got the nickname Crazy Judah for this idea. But he didn't let that stop him. In 1860 he found a mountain pass that made crossing the range much easier.

Theodore Judah

Judah also started searching for men with the power and the money to form and help fund a railroad company. The company would become the Central Pacific Railroad. The men he chose were called the Big Four: Charles Crocker, Collis Huntington, Mark Hopkins, and Leland Stanford. Then Judah talked to Washington lawmakers. He said that the Central Pacific should build eastward from California. It would form the western link of the transcontinental railroad.

Crisis and Progress

One important American who wanted a railroad to the Pacific was President Abraham Lincoln. Like many others, Lincoln believed that train travel was the key to a bright future for business, trade, and culture in the United States. However, Lincoln soon had to face more urgent matters.

Between December 1860 and June 1861, eleven states in the South seceded from the United States. These states broke away over the issue of slavery and other disagreements with the North. They founded a new, separate government called the Confederate States of America. States in the North, still led by President Lincoln, became known as the Union. Lincoln refused to accept the South's secession. The US Civil War began in April 1861.

President Abraham Lincoln

The war deeply damaged the country. Sometimes family members were on opposite sides of the battle lines. Hundreds of thousands of people died.

Yet the war also opened a door for the railroad. Confederate lawmakers did not vote in Congress. So Union politicians finally settled the debate about the railroad's path. On July 1, 1862, Congress passed the Pacific Railway Act.

That law created the Union Pacific Railroad. This new company would be in charge of building the railroad westward. The government would choose a group of people to set up the company and decide who would run it. The act said the

Central Pacific would work on the railroad too. It would start in California and go east. Eventually the two companies would meet and connect the railroad's two parts. The act also said that if the work did not move fast enough, the government could step in and take control of profits made by the railroad when it was finished.

Money Matters

With the route decided, another key question remained: Who would pay for the railroad—and how? The US government controlled most of the land the railroad would cross. But it did not want to pay for all the materials, labor, and other costs. So lawmakers agreed on a plan to give the railroad companies land to build on. The government would also give the companies a certain amount of land next to the railroad for each mile of track they built. The companies would then own this land and could sell some of it if they wanted to.

Union politicians created the Pacific Railway Act to resolve the debate surrounding the railroad's route.

The government also pledged to give the companies loans in the form of government bonds. The railroad companies would then use these bonds to fund construction. Later, they would need to pay back the government loans. But in the meantime, they expected to earn plenty of money by operating the railroads, selling stock in the railroad companies, and selling some of the land they received from the government.

The law also said that the railway companies would build telegraph lines along the railroad track. Before the telephone was invented in 1876, the telegraph was the fastest form of long-distance communication. The telegraph line would help

During the railroad's construction, telegraph lines were built to help railroad companies and new settlers communicate over long distances.

the railroad companies keep investors and the general public informed about the railroad's progress. It would also give the United States a greater communication network as more settlers moved west.

The Pacific Railway Act said that railroad construction would start from two cities at opposite ends of the future line. In the West, the Central Pacific Railroad would begin work in Sacramento, California. The Central Pacific would build over the Sierra Nevada to the western boundary of the Nevada Territory. The Union Pacific Railroad would begin along the Missouri River and build west. (To the east, the Union Pacific would also connect to tracks that already ran to the Atlantic Ocean.) According to this plan, the two companies' tracks would meet up somewhere near the Nevada-California border.

After more than thirty years of debate, work on the transcontinental railroad was finally going to begin.

The Pacific Railway Act said that the new tracks of the transcontinental railroad would stretch from Sacramento, California, to the Missouri River.

CHAPTER 3

THE GREAT PROJECT BEGINS

1800   **1860**   **1861**   **1862**

1800s: Thousands of people immigrate to the United States from countries including Ireland, Italy, Germany, and China.

At long last, the government had chosen a path for the railroad. The government had chosen the companies that would oversee building that railroad. But how would the railroad actually get built? And who were the workers who would take on this huge job?

How to Build a Railroad

Building the railroad took many steps and many teams of workers. First, surveyors went on ahead and chose the exact path. The general route was already set. But surveyors looked at the details. If they found anything that would make it harder to lay tracks, they made small changes to the route.

Once the path was chosen, the land had to be graded. Grading teams built a raised bed of earth to lay the tracks on.

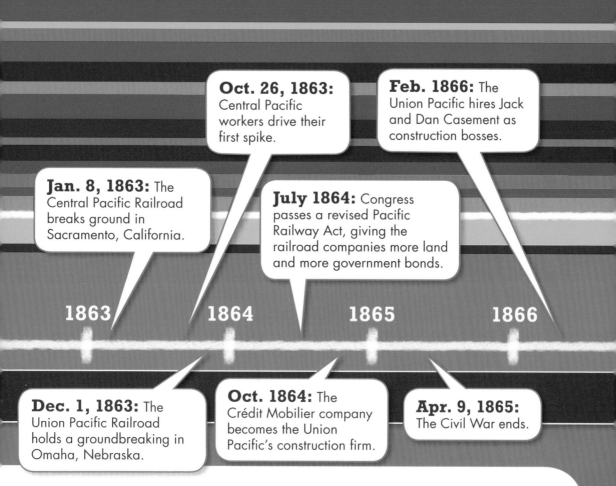

Oct. 26, 1863: Central Pacific workers drive their first spike.

Feb. 1866: The Union Pacific hires Jack and Dan Casement as construction bosses.

Jan. 8, 1863: The Central Pacific Railroad breaks ground in Sacramento, California.

July 1864: Congress passes a revised Pacific Railway Act, giving the railroad companies more land and more government bonds.

1863   1864   1865   1866

Dec. 1, 1863: The Union Pacific Railroad holds a groundbreaking in Omaha, Nebraska.

Oct. 1864: The Crédit Mobilier company becomes the Union Pacific's construction firm.

Apr. 9, 1865: The Civil War ends.

This grade stood a couple of feet aboveground. It was about 12 feet (4 meters) across, wide enough for two sets of side-by-side tracks. Graders dug up earth with shovels and pickaxes. These workers used wheelbarrows to move the dirt to the grade. They dumped the dirt wherever the team boss told them to. The boss smoothed the earth with a shovel. If a shovel couldn't do the job, horses or oxen pulled heavy scrapers to flatten the grade.

Next, workers laid down railroad ties. These thick wooden planks were about 6 feet (1.8 m) long. Then it was time to lay down the rails. Made of iron, the rails weighed hundreds of pounds. Workers laid them across the ties. And finally, workers used sledgehammers to pound spikes into the rails and ties. The spikes would hold everything in place.

Workers from around the World

Building the railroad was hard work, but it was also steady work. And the pay was not bad for that time.

Many people who worked on the railroad were new to the country. In the early and mid-nineteenth century, thousands of people moved to the United States from other nations. These immigrants left their homes for many reasons. Many had lived in poverty. Some were not allowed to follow their religions. Others faced war or other violence. All hoped to find better lives and brighter futures in the United States. In the eastern states, many immigrants were Irish, Italian, and German. Out west, most new arrivals were from China.

Immigrants faced hardships in their new home. Many arrived with little or no money. Paying for housing was hard. Large families shared very small apartments. Living conditions were often poor.

Many immigrants from China were hired to help build the transcontinental railroad.

People in the United States often discriminated against these new arrivals. Most immigrants did not speak English. Their religions, foods, and other customs sometimes seemed unfamiliar to other people in the United States. Some people were suspicious of anyone whose appearance was different from their own. Immigrants were often treated badly because of their clothing or skin color.

For these reasons, it was also hard for some immigrants to find jobs. New arrivals who could find work often worked long hours for little pay. So when the railroad building began, many immigrants were eager to be part of it.

Breaking Ground

The Central Pacific broke ground in Sacramento on January 8, 1863. This ceremony officially marked the beginning of work on the railroad. But in fact, the first step in the project was already in progress. Workers were building a bridge across the nearby American River. A steam-powered machine was driving huge wooden posts into the riverbed. These posts would support the bridge. The machine made a huge pounding noise that boomed over the ceremony's speeches. But that noise was a welcome sign of progress.

On January 8, 1863, observers gathered for the groundbreaking ceremony in Sacramento, celebrating the official start of construction on the transcontinental railroad.

Not much more would happen for a while, though. Building the bridge took time. And the railroad company was having money problems. It needed to raise more funds to pay for workers and materials. But on October 26, 1863, Central Pacific laborers finally drove the first spike on the track.

It was an important step. And in the spring and early summer of 1865, workers began the long, slow climb into the Sierra Nevada.

Delays and Deals

Near the end of 1863, Lincoln officially chose Omaha, Nebraska, as the starting point of the Union Pacific Railroad. On December 1, the company held a ceremony there. A month later, the Union Pacific chose Peter Dey as chief engineer. Former New York senator John Dix was the Union Pacific's president.

After many delays, railroad workers began laying down rails and tracks in late 1863.

Like the Central Pacific, the Union Pacific faced delays right away. Months passed before workers actually laid any rails. First, the exact route out of Omaha had to be changed. The original route was too hilly. Problems with materials caused another delay. Workers had used railroad ties made of wood that was too soft. So the company had to bring in harder ties from states back east. Slow-moving wagons had to carry the ties and other materials to the workers. With these delays, the Union Pacific had finished only 11 miles (18 kilometers) of track by September 25, 1865.

Another part of the Union Pacific's trouble was its leader. John Dix was officially president. But a businessman named Thomas C. Durant was making the real decisions.

Durant made deals with the government for more land and loans. He found more investors to provide money for construction. Meanwhile, he started his own construction company, Crédit Mobilier. Then, in his role with the Union Pacific, he hired Crédit Mobilier to build the railroad. Basically, Durant paid himself with the money from investors and the government. Other Union Pacific leaders joined Durant in this clever scam. They wanted a piece of the profits too.

Thomas C. Durant

New Workers on the Job

Work was gradually gaining speed for the Union Pacific. Much of that work was done by Irish laborers and bosses. About one-third of Union Pacific workers came from Ireland. Crews also included some German, Italian, Dutch, and Czech immigrants.

On April 9, 1865, the Civil War ended. The North had won. Many men who had fought in the war were looking for work. And the Union Pacific was looking for more workers. Former Civil War officers and engineers took leadership roles. And lower-ranking soldiers joined the hard labor crews. The Union Pacific also hired African American men who had been enslaved in the South but had been freed by the Union's victory in the war.

Many workers joining the project had never built a railroad before. But they learned fast. The Union Pacific finally began to make real progress across the plains.

Culture Clash and Common Ground

Like the Union Pacific, the Central Pacific hired many Irish American workers. But the company had trouble finding and

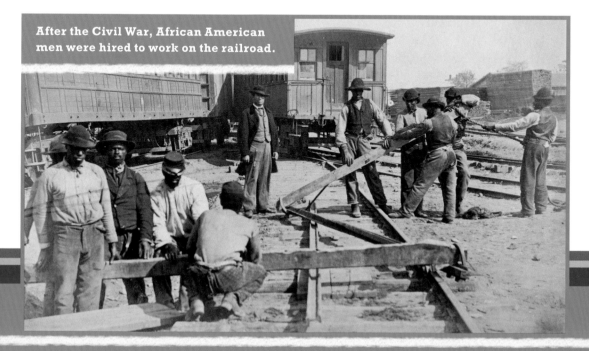

After the Civil War, African American men were hired to work on the railroad.

keeping enough workers. Some went on strike. They refused to work until they got more money. Others left for jobs in the gold and silver mines. So by 1865, the Central Pacific had begun to hire more and more Chinese immigrants to build the railroad. The Central Pacific sent out scouts to recruit Chinese workers in California. They also began advertising in China. Thousands of Chinese workers answered the call.

The Irish and Chinese workers didn't always get along. They spoke different languages. They ate different foods. And they earned different pay. While Chinese workers' wages went up over time, they were still lower than the wages earned by the Irish and other white workers.

Despite all of these differences, the Central Pacific's workers lived similar lives in other ways. Formed into groups organized by task, they worked long days. They often put in more than twelve hours of hard labor at a time. At night they ate dinner and bedded down in tents along the ever-lengthening tracks. And then they got up and started working again.

Railroad workers of different ethnicities did not always get along, but their daily lives were similar.

Over, around, and through the Mountains

In their journey over the Sierra Nevada, Central Pacific workers had to move a lot of rock out of the railroad's path. To do this, they became skilled at using an explosive mixture called black powder. They drilled holes into stone and stuffed in the powder. Then they lit a fuse to cause an explosion.

Armed with this tool, workers faced the two biggest challenges of the Sierra Nevada: Cape Horn and Summit Peak. Workers arrived at Cape Horn in the fall of 1865. Cape Horn was a tall, sheer cliff. It would be too hard to build a tunnel through it. Instead, workers carved a track right into the side of the mountain. First, to reach the cliff's face, Chinese workers used reeds to weave baskets big enough to hold people. They attached ropes to these baskets. Then Chinese laborers climbed inside. Other laborers used the ropes to lower the baskets down the side of the cliff. The workers used black powder to blast holes in the rock. After lighting the fuse, they had only a few moments to get away before the explosion. The laborers had to trust the workers above to haul up the baskets in time.

Bit by bit, this dangerous process made

Central Pacific workers carve a track into the side of Cape Horn.

a narrow ledge going around the mountain. Next, workers stood on this shelf of land and used pickaxes to make it wider. Finally, the ledge was big enough for tracks to be laid. The Cape Horn project took a year.

Summit Peak was another hurdle. It was too high to go over. It was also too steep to cut a ledge into. The only way forward was to go through it. The solid granite of the mountains was extremely hard. It took a long time to make progress using black powder. So the Central Pacific attacked the rock with something stronger: nitroglycerin. In the 1860s, this explosive liquid was a relatively new discovery. It was very powerful. It was also very dangerous. Workers were sometimes badly injured or even killed in explosions.

By the time the railroad was complete, Central Pacific workers would carve a total of fifteen tunnels. But the Summit Tunnel was the longest and most difficult. It took fifteen months to build it. When the tunnel was finished, it was 1,659 feet (506 m) long.

Workers used dangerous explosives to create the Summit Tunnel.

Deeper into the West

Compared to the Central Pacific's path, the Union Pacific had much easier, flatter land to cross. But as workers moved across the plains, they also moved farther into lands once controlled by American Indians. Clashes sometimes erupted. Some regional tribes stole horses, food, and other goods from railroad camps. Sometimes warriors attacked and killed settlers or workers in the region. These American Indians were often defending themselves against the settlers who were taking over their land and forcing them to adopt new ways of life.

At other times, the fear of attack was larger than the actual risk. This fear sometimes led white settlers and workers to attack American Indians first. Violent actions were taken by both sides.

Casement's Army

In February 1866, the Union Pacific hired brothers Jack and Dan Casement as construction bosses. Together the Casements put together a workforce and a system that became known as Casement's Army.

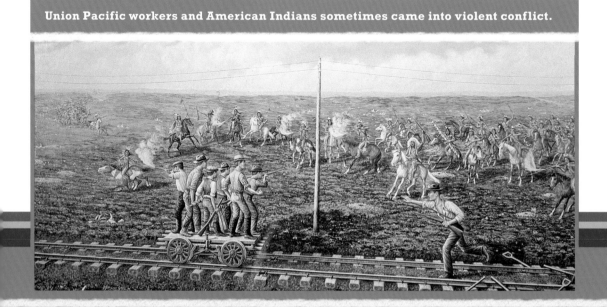
Union Pacific workers and American Indians sometimes came into violent conflict.

A key part of the Casement brothers' system was the supply train. This train traveled along the track that workers had just built. It carried tools and materials to the end of the line. That way the supplies were ready as soon as workers needed them. The Casement brothers also used a train car as a traveling blacksmith shop. Blacksmiths fixed tools and made new horseshoes. (Horses were also working hard pulling supply wagons.)

Jack and Dan Casement knew it was important to motivate their workers. They promised rewards such as extra pay if their teams laid a certain amount of track in a day. It worked. The crews often built a mile (1.6 km) a day or more. In its first twenty months, the Union Pacific had only laid 11 miles (18 km). The Casement brothers seemed like miracle workers.

The Union Pacific had one more important post to fill. In 1865 Peter Dey had quit as chief engineer. So in spring 1866, the Union Pacific hired Grenville Dodge to take over the position. Dodge was a railroad engineer and Civil War veteran. And he was about to enter the race of his life.

ROOM AND BOARD

The Casements set up one car on their supply train to serve as a kitchen and a cafeteria. One train's dining car had a table where 125 hungry workers could sit and eat simple but hearty meals. There were also sleeping cars full of bunk beds. But the close quarters often became infested with lice. Some workers pitched tents away from the tracks instead of using these bunks.

CHAPTER 4

THE RACE

1866–1867: Winter brings terrible storms to both crews, slowing down work on the railroad.

JAN. 1866   **JULY 1866**   **JAN. 1867**   **JULY 1867**

June 1866: The US government allows the Central Pacific to keep working eastward past the Nevada border.

Jan. 1867: The Central Pacific battles dangerous avalanches in the mountains.

In June 1866, government officials decided on a change in plans. They wanted the railroad finished as soon as possible. Even with the Casement Army marching over the plains, the Union Pacific still had a long way to go. Central Pacific officials wanted the chance to keep building past the Nevada-California boundary the Pacific Railway Act had set as a limit. They hadn't gotten to that point yet. But Central Pacific officials were sure their own workers would get there before the Union Pacific could. So the government decided to let the Central Pacific keep working until the two lines met. Both companies knew that every mile they built earned them more land and more profits. The race was on.

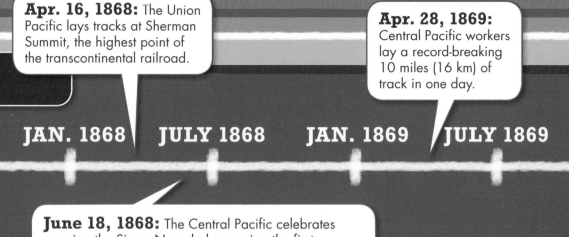

Apr. 16, 1868: The Union Pacific lays tracks at Sherman Summit, the highest point of the transcontinental railroad.

Apr. 28, 1869: Central Pacific workers lay a record-breaking 10 miles (16 km) of track in one day.

JAN. 1868 **JULY 1868** **JAN. 1869** **JULY 1869**

June 18, 1868: The Central Pacific celebrates crossing the Sierra Nevada by running the first passenger train across the mountains to Reno, Nevada.

Fighting Mother Nature

The race would pit the railroad companies against each other. The companies also had to face another tough foe: the weather. The winter of 1866–1867 brought terrible storms to the West. In February 1867, a huge blizzard struck the Union Pacific in western Nebraska. It lasted a week. Work came to a screeching halt. A few days after the storm ended, another one buried the region in snow. Even when the worst of winter was over, the snow made trouble. As it melted, the water flowed downhill. Sometimes it caused flooding.

The same season brought awful weather to the Sierra Nevada in California. As late as April, storms were dropping up to 5 feet (1.5 m) of snow. And high in the mountains, the building season was short. The snow began falling again in September 1867. It would be another brutal winter.

Life along the Line

Along the Union Pacific's tracks, from Nebraska to Wyoming, new settlements sprang up where none had been around for many miles. As workers moved into a new area and made camp, restaurants, saloons, gambling houses, and dance halls set up shop nearby. Many times, when the workers moved on, so did the settlements. These traveling communities were often home to rough customers and bad behavior.

Not all the communities that grew along the tracks disappeared, though. The Wyoming towns of Cheyenne and Laramie, for instance, were both founded alongside the railroad. Both lived on to be thriving modern cities.

Cold weather and snow made it difficult to work on the railroad.

Up to the Rockies

The Central Pacific workers had been working in the mountains for years. But the Union Pacific didn't face this kind of obstacle until April 1868, when they hit the Rocky Mountains. In Colorado the Rockies rise to heights of over 14,000 feet (4,270 m). But in Wyoming, they are lower and rise less steeply. In fact, the Union Pacific team had been steadily climbing in elevation ever since it left Omaha. The railroad's route had been chosen to make it as easy as possible to cross the Rockies.

As the tracks headed down from South Pass, the Wyoming town where the rails crossed the Rockies, the Union Pacific found new trouble. For many miles to the west, the land had no water that was safe to drink—at least not on the surface. Workers drilled wells. But they still did not find water. So once again, the new track itself was the solution. Trains carried water along the tracks to workers. Then they headed back east for more.

Down into the Desert

In spring 1868, the Union Pacific headed over the Rockies. And the Central Pacific had finally crossed the Sierra Nevada. The tracks headed down the other side into Nevada. Workers were relieved to be on flat ground.

TOWERING BRIDGES

Along with blasting tunnels, the railways had to build bridges. The Union Pacific's longest bridge was the Dale Creek Bridge. West of Sherman, Wyoming, the bridge was around 700 feet (213 m) long and stood more than 120 feet (37 m) high. The Central Pacific's most impressive bridge was Long Ravine Bridge, in the Sierra Nevada. It stretched more than 875 feet (267 m) and was 120 feet (37 m) high.

But this flat ground was also a desert. In the summer, it was very hot. Temperatures could get up to 120°F (49°C). And the barren land provided few supplies. There were no trees to cut down and make into boards. Materials had to come from farther west. Trains brought them into the desert on the brand-new tracks.

And of course, the desert also lacked water. Central Pacific engineers thought it would be too hard to dig wells deep enough to reach water they could drink. Instead, workers drilled into the rock of the mountains they'd just crossed. They tapped springs there.

On June 18, 1868, the Central Pacific celebrated a big success. That day the first passenger train crossed the Sierra Nevada and traveled to Reno, Nevada. Even in June, there was still a lot of snow high in the mountains. From this snowy peak, the train traveled down into the baking desert.

From Reno the tracks turned northeast across Nevada toward Utah. The Central Pacific was in a hurry to meet the Union Pacific there.

This map shows both the Central Pacific and Union Pacific railway lines.

Breakneck Speed

As the finish line grew closer, quality sometimes suffered. The railroad owners were in a rush to win the race. So they were willing to look the other way when workers used softer wood for ties or weren't as careful in their work.

Meanwhile, the pressure was on to build faster than ever. Some stories say Charles Crocker of the Central Pacific bet Thomas Durant of the Union Pacific $10,000 that the Central Pacific's workers could build 10 miles (16 km) of track in a single day. No one is sure if the bet really happened. But one thing is certain. On April 28, 1869, the Central Pacific made history. That day, workers laid 10 miles—plus more than 50 feet (15 m) extra.

When the day began, the land ahead had already been graded. Early that morning, workers quickly unloaded train cars full of supplies. A team of eight Irishmen placed the rails. With amazing speed, they laid two rails every twelve seconds. At the end of the day, the Central Pacific had put down more than twenty-five thousand ties, three thousand rails, and twenty-eight thousand spikes.

On April 28, 1869, Central Pacific workers laid more than 10 miles (16 km) of railroad track.

CHAPTER 5

THE GOLDEN SPIKE AND BEYOND

Oct. 1871: A mob attacks Chinatown in Los Angeles, leaving at least eighteen Chinese immigrants dead.

Apr. 1869: Congress passes a law making Promontory, Utah, the site where the Central Pacific and the Union Pacific will meet.

1860   1865   1870   1875

May 10, 1869: Railroad officials drive the last spikes of the transcontinental railroad at Promontory, Utah. The finished railroad is 1,776 miles (2,858 km) long.

1872: The Crédit Mobilier scandal erupts.

By spring 1869, both the Union Pacific and the Central Pacific were crossing northern Utah. They were closing in on each other and the end of the race.

But where exactly would the tracks meet? The Central Pacific and the Union Pacific both wanted to finish as many miles as they could. That would mean that they got more land, more government bonds, and more profit from the operating railroad. So both companies just kept building.

The race had to end. The government stepped in. It tried to convince the companies to compromise with each other. But neither one wanted to budge. In early April, they finally reached an agreement. Congress quickly made it official with a special law. The line would join at Promontory, Utah.

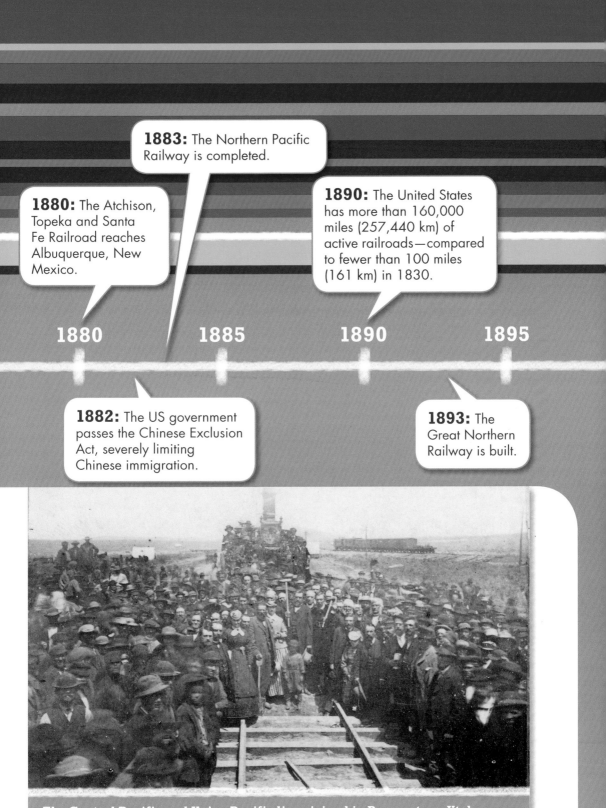

1883: The Northern Pacific Railway is completed.

1880: The Atchison, Topeka and Santa Fe Railroad reaches Albuquerque, New Mexico.

1890: The United States has more than 160,000 miles (257,440 km) of active railroads—compared to fewer than 100 miles (161 km) in 1830.

1880   1885   1890   1895

1882: The US government passes the Chinese Exclusion Act, severely limiting Chinese immigration.

1893: The Great Northern Railway is built.

The Central Pacific and Union Pacific lines joined in Promontory, Utah.

The Last Rail Is Laid

On May 10, 1869, two locomotives sat facing each other. One was from the Union Pacific, and one was from the Central Pacific. Between them, two last rails had to be placed.

A crowd was gathered at Promontory to see the historic event. As they watched, a team from the Central Pacific carried the final rails to the track. They also brought a special railroad tie. Two Central Pacific construction bosses laid the tie. Then the workers placed the rails and drove in spikes.

Next, Thomas Durant of the Union Pacific drove in a spike. Finally, only one last spike remained. This special spike was made of California gold. It had been crafted just for this occasion. Leland Stanford of the Central Pacific would have the honor of placing it. He swung a sledgehammer, like thousands of his workers had for the last six years. Stanford wasn't so experienced with the work, though. He missed the spike and hit the rail. But the crowd hardly cared. At last, the great railroad was built!

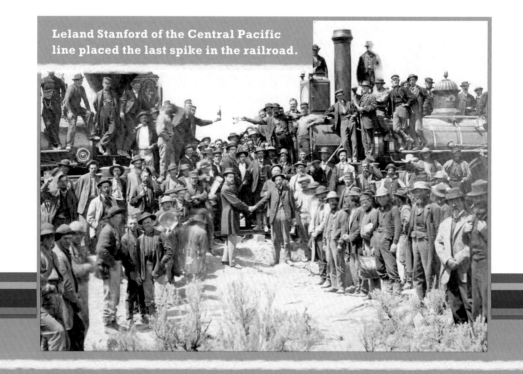

Leland Stanford of the Central Pacific line placed the last spike in the railroad.

After the Ceremony

When the transcontinental railroad opened to passengers, it took just a week to cross the United States. That trip had once taken at least six months across land. And it had taken six weeks by water. People were eager to make the historic journey. Riders came not only from the United States but also from other nations. Travelers were impressed by this new railroad.

As expected, the railroad cut costs for travel and shipping goods. And the telegraph lines that ran beside the track made American communication faster and easier than ever before.

Railroad building didn't stop. By 1880 the Atchison, Topeka and Santa Fe Railroad had reached Albuquerque, New Mexico, connecting it to Independence, Missouri. Two railroads were also built across the northern United States. They stretched from Minnesota to what would become Washington State. In 1883 the Northern Pacific Railway was finished. The Great Northern Railway followed in 1893. Other new railroad companies were building tracks all over the nation.

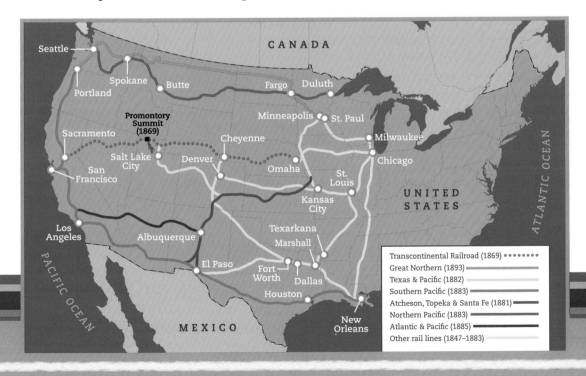

CANADA

Seattle
Spokane Butte   Fargo Duluth
Portland
                                Minneapolis St. Paul
Promontory
Summit
(1869)
Sacramento   Cheyenne   Milwaukee
Salt Lake   Denver   Chicago
San   City   Omaha
Francisco   St.
                                 Louis   UNITED
                              Kansas   STATES
                               City
Los   Texarkana
Angeles   Albuquerque   Marshall
                El Paso   Fort
                              Worth Dallas
                              Houston
                                        New
                                        Orleans
MEXICO

PACIFIC OCEAN

ATLANTIC OCEAN

Transcontinental Railroad (1869) ●●●●●●●
Great Northern (1893)
Texas & Pacific (1882)
Southern Pacific (1883)
Atcheson, Topeka & Santa Fe (1881)
Northern Pacific (1883)
Atlantic & Pacific (1885)
Other rail lines (1847–1883)

But not everything was positive or peaceful. In 1872 a Senate investigation set off the Crédit Mobilier scandal. The investigation exposed that Thomas Durant and other Union Pacific leaders had been dishonest in using money from investors and the government. The scandal damaged the honor of some of the country's most powerful men.

The end of the railroad also put a lot of people out of work. Finding new jobs was especially hard for thousands of Chinese workers. Most of them headed to California looking for work. But they faced greater discrimination than ever—and even violence. In October 1871, hundreds of white people entered Chinatown in Los Angeles and attacked residents. At least eighteen immigrants were killed. And in 1882, the US government passed the Chinese Exclusion Act. This law closed the door to most Chinese immigrants. It also made it hard for immigrants already living to the country to become US citizens. The law was repealed in 1943.

The railroad also brought greater hardship for American Indians. More and more new people flooded into lands that had once been theirs. Conflict with white settlers continued.

Chinatown in Los Angeles, 1890

Many American Indians were forced off their lands. They had to leave their homes—and often their traditions—behind. Many died traveling to reservations. In modern times, many American Indians still live on reservations. On many of these reservations, living conditions are difficult. Jobs can be hard to find. Both on and off reservations, American Indians often face discrimination. Many struggle to stay connected to their cultures.

The story of the transcontinental railroad and its effects is not simple. Yet along with the troubles it brought, the railroad had deep and lasting positive results. Many people in the United States saw parts of their country they had never imagined. They met people they would never have known otherwise. And with the railroad's help, they created a new vision of the vast and diverse nation they shared.

Building the transcontinental railroad was a long and difficult process, but it led to great improvements for travel and communication within the United States.

Writing Activity

Imagine that you are an immigrant who moved to the United States to work on the transcontinental railroad, either with the Central Pacific or the Union Pacific. What would your life be like? What would each day bring? What would your most exciting, difficult, scary, and joyful experiences be?

Choose an event from one of the railroad's timelines that interests you. Imagine that you saw this event or heard about it. Then, as that railroad worker, write a letter about this event to a family member or a friend back home. As you write, think about questions such as these:

How did you feel about the event?

What did you do in response to the event?

What surprised you most about this event?

Was your life different after this event?

What do you think the long-term effects of this event will be?

What is the one most important thing you want to tell a family member or a friend back home about this event?

Glossary

discrimination: unfair treatment of a person or a group of people based on characteristics such as race or ethnicity

engineer: a person who designs and builds complicated machines, structures, or systems

government bond: a government-issued document that can be purchased and, after a certain amount of time, can be sold back to the government for the purchase price plus interest

groundbreaking: a ceremony celebrating the beginning of a building project

investor: someone who shares the cost and risk of a company or a project but also shares in its profits or rewards

locomotive: the part of a train that produces power and pulls the rest of the train

nitroglycerin: an explosive liquid

relocation: moving or being moved to a new place

reservation: an area of land set aside by the US government for American Indians to live on

secede: to leave a nation

survey: to examine and measure an area of land; a report after surveying land

telegraph: a communication system that used electrical signals to send messages along a wire

treaty: a written agreement between two or more governments or groups

Further Information

Nardo, Don. *The Golden Spike: How a Photograph Celebrated the Transcontinental Railroad.* North Mankato, MN: Compass Point, 2015. This book uses a famous photograph of the golden spike to explore the meeting of the Central Pacific and the Union Pacific lines.

Our Documents
http://www.ourdocuments.gov/doc.php?flash=true&doc=32
Visit this site to see a picture of the original Pacific Railway Act.

Roza, Greg. *Westward Expansion.* New York: Gareth Stevens, 2011. This book explores the reasons many Americans moved west in the nineteenth century.

Sheinkin, Steve. *Which Way to the Wild West? Everything Your Schoolbooks Didn't Tell You about Westward Expansion.* New York: Roaring Brook, 2009. This book offers surprising facts about America's westward expansion.

Stein, R. Conrad. *The Incredible Transcontinental Railroad.* Berkeley Heights, NJ: Enslow, 2012. Learn more about the construction of the transcontinental railroad and how it helped transform the West.

The Transcontinental Railroad
http://www.pbs.org/wgbh/americanexperience/films/tcrr/
This website from PBS explores the people, the places, and the events connected to the transcontinental railroad.

LERNER
SOURCE™

Expand learning beyond the printed book. Download free, complementary educational resources for this book from our website, www.lerneresource.com.

Index

Photo Acknowledgments

The images in this book are used with the permission of: Library of Congress, pp. 5 (LC-DIG-ppmsca-07295), 13 (98688480), 14 (LC-DIG-stereo-1s00538), 16 (LC-USZ62-5876), 26 (LC-DIG-ppmsca-10397), 29 ((LC-DIG-stereo-2s00547), 36 (98688841); © American Stock/Archive Photos/Getty Images, p. 8; The Granger Collection, New York, pp. 12, 22, 27; © California State Railroad Museum Library, p. 15; National Archives, pp. 17, 25 (1135962), 40 (594940); © Otto Herschan/Hulton Archive/Getty Images, p. 18; California State Railroad Museum via Waymark.com, p. 23; Robert N. Dennis collection of stereoscopic views/United States/Subject series/Railroads/Central Pacific Railroad, Miriam and Ira D. Wallach Division of Art, Prints and Photographs, The New York Public Library, Astor, Lenox and Tilden Foundations, pp.24, 34; © Ivy Close Images/Alamy, p. 28; © Gogolin, Jacob (1864-1940) (after)/Private Collection/Peter Newark American Pictures/Bridgeman Images, p. 30; © Linda Hall Library, p. 37; The Huntington Library, San Marino, CA, p. 39; © Laura Westlund/Independent Picture Service, p. 41, Robert N. Dennis collection of stereoscopic views/Stephen A. Schwarzman Building/Photography Collection, Miriam and Ira D. Wallach Division of Art, Prints and Photographs, p. 42; © Track-layers gang-building the Union Pacific Railroad through American wilderness, 1860s (b/w photo), American Photographer, (19th century)/Private Collection /Peter Newark American Pictures/Bridgeman Images, p. 43.

Front cover: Library of Congress (LC-DIG-stereo-1s00618).

Main text font set in Caecilia Com 55 Roman 11/16.
Typeface provided by Linotype AG.